THE FACTS OF NUTRITION

HILTON H

THE FACTS OF NUTRITION

By

Prof. Hilton Hotema

ISBN: 978-1-64093-016-2

Published by:
Orkos Press
P.O. Box 2085
Astoria New York 11102

Also by Hilton Hotema:

The Great Law

Why Do We Die

The Genesis of Christianity

Mystery of Man

The Great Red Dragon

Contents

The Magic Cell

In Part II of our work titled Pre-Existence of Man, we have shown that the beginning and the development of the human body result from cells which are composed of atoms and not of food.

In fact, in the work of the cells, we come into contact with Cosmic Consciousness, but the doctors fail to realize it. And it further appears that Cosmic Consciousness is a quality which is inherent in the ions, electrons, atoms and molecules of which the cells are composed.

Magic is a term of Occult Science. It is the art of activating the power of the Creative Principle of the Universe.

Magic is a word well applied to the production and maintenance of Man. The process is so strange and so foreign to anything modern science teaches, that it will be many years yet before the process will be recognized and recorded in the text-books—if ever.

For to recognize publicly the actual facts as to the production and maintenance of Man would explode every medical theory, as the theories of medical art are based on erroneous assumptions and not on actual facts.

In the work of the Creative Process appears all the magic and mystery that can be attributed only to Spiritual Forces; and physical science declares that such forces do not exist.

We will agree with that too; but we cannot discount the fact that there are forces at work in the Universe which physical science cannot disregard, but which it refuses to recognize. In its attempt to disregard them, it invents such preposterous theories as those appertaining to the animation of the body, that Life is the expression of a series of chemical changes (Osler).

We shall observe one simple operation of the Creative Principle. It is well known that water is formed of invisible atoms. By merely lowering the temperature, change to ice. Then the ice changes back to invisible vapor by simply raising the temperature, which increases the vibrations of the atoms and they become invisible to us.

That is the regular operation of the Creative Process, not only in one case, but in all cases, from the production of ice to the production of man.

It just takes more time to make man of invisible elements and return him to invisible elements, and yet that process is occurring constantly. But when man returns to invisible elements, that does not mean the end of Life, nor the end of man, as we have sown in Pre-Existence of Man.

Living things appear to reproduce themselves. That is an illusion. The same may be said of water and ice. It is the work of the Creative

Principle, guided by Infinite Intelligence which inheres in the elements of Creation.

As to man, the creative process appears to be accomplished by the work of the Parent Cell, in which the Element of Existence seems to begin its work.

Here is the point where modern science gets lost. According to Berman, the Creative Process seems to work like this:

"Our chemical factory consists of cells, manufacturing special substances that act upon the other cells of the body, and so start and determine the countless processes that we call life. Life, body and soul emerge from the activity of the magic ooze of their silent chemistry." The absurdity of that assertion appears by simply asking –"Which came first, the cells of the chemical factory, or the substances which they make?"

Berman's factory consists of cells, but he deems it unimportant to explain where, when, or how he gets them. That is a common example of what is termed science. It is tragic when we consider the calamitous results arising from such "scientific" nonsense.

According to the "childish physico-chemical conceptions" of science, as Carrel termed them, the living organism is the product of food and is sustained by food. In the light of recent discoveries, this "science" of the 19th century "must be abandoned," continued Carrel.

Food Does Not Produce The Body

Biologists show that the organism is not the product of food, nor is it sustained by food.

Food and drink are required only as the occasion and condition that bring into action the vital processes that manufacture, from invisible substance, the atomic products that build, sustain repair, and vitalize the organism. That is the reason why medical art knows nothing about "vital energy" and the process of nutrition within the organism.

Nothing can sustain that which it cannot produce. If the living organism is not the product of food and drink, it is not sustained by these.

Sadly do scientists miss the mark when they seek for the sustaining power of Life and Health in things beneath them. Food and drink are only the occasion and condition for the operation of the Productive Process. But their sustaining and vitalizing power is a fiction of medical minds.

Edison had a plant that condensed nitrates from the air. They were sacked and sold to farmers for fertilizer. We put some lead in a pot on a hot stove, and in time the metal boiled away and vanished. What had been heavy lead was now invisible gas floating in the air.

The body is composed of trillions of cells. Each cell, according to science, comes from the original Parent Cell; but in *The Pre-Existence of Man,* we have shown that this is erroneous.

As the Transformative Principle produces water, ice and metal from invisible gases, in like manner it produces the Primary Cell and all the cells that follow. All qualities of the Productive Principle pass on to the Primary Cell and all the following cells, in character if not in degree.

The Primary Cell and all the cells that follow are composed of atoms so small that 900,000 of them could set side by side on a pin point.

A cubic millimeter of human blood contains about five million red corpuscles. A molecule of the corpuscle contains more than 100 atoms; and molecules are so small that they are too tiny to reflect visible light. Hence they must be forever invisible to us.

If the molecules in a thimbleful of water were each magnified to the size of an orange, they would cover the entire United States with a layer of orange 1,000 feet deep.

The 100 or more atoms in each of these tiny molecules are globular system in which electrons, protons, neutrons, etc., revolve with lightning speed around their common center of attraction, like the planets and the sun of our solar system.

The human body is a mass of trillions of cells. Each cell is a mass of millions of atoms, each of which is a globular system with "planets" whirling with tremendous speed.

What use, asks the biologist, has such a system for food and drink? What use has the solar system for food and drink? We have on file a record of cases of persons who have gone without food from forty days to forty years.

As the cells of the body all come from the Primary Cell, they inherit all the qualities of that cell which it inherits from the Productive Principle, including Intelligence. So man's Intelligence comes thru his cells, direct from the Primary Source. This Infinite Intelligence is limited in man because of his limited capacity to receive and exhibit it.

The reason why most men show so little intelligence is due to the fact that the process of training and educating is designed to fill the mind with false theories that drive out all the Natural Intelligence.

As we trace upward in the scale of living things, from the unicellular organism, the phenomenon of development appears. The one-celled amoeba comes into being from a previous amoeba, and not from food and drink.

In the higher organisms, each Being begins as a single cell and develops by cell division. Food and drink are not the developing agents.

The cells come from the division of preceding cells, and all adhere to one differentiated community that ultimately forms the complex but co-ordinated whole, the human body.

The details of cell construction and division are a longer story than is necessary for our purpose. The two points involved here are—

1. The original cell, which begins the formation of man, exhibits that uncanny Intelligence which is inherent in the atom, and
2. That cell does not come from food, and does not depend on food. As the law does not change, the rest of the cells do not come from food and do not depend on food for their maintenance. Yet it seems that they do, just as the sun seems to rise. It is all an illusions.

The Productive Process never changes. It does not start in one direction, then change to another. As the organism begins as a cell and develops by reason of cell division, so the whole body, only a mass of cells, is maintained during its existence by the same process.

The Primary Cell that begins the formation of man, appears to result from the union of the male and female germ cells. That union appears to constitute the occasion and condition that bring the Productive Principle into action to bring into being the Magic Cell that begins the existence of man.

This primary beginning is very mysterious and little understood. On this point Carver writes:

"The germinal elements separate into their particles, and the general cytoplasm of the ovum, as it is called, begins to be organized with relation to what are now called the pronucleus and the female pro-nucleus, and as this arrangement occurs, the gametes or pro-nuclei travel toward each other. As they come near to each other, certain elements of each stand out separately, and, coming nearer, these separate, individual particles merge and fuse, as it were, into each other, producing a clear field in which nothing appears. Finally, after a period of seeming quiescence, granulation occurs at the point between the places occupied by the gametes when they disappeared from sight.

"The granulated point is the beginning of the new person, and is called the Zygote or pre-embryo, the production of which completes the period of impregnation" (Psycho-Bio-Physiology).

The male and female gametes meet and fuse; they disappear from sight, leaving a clear field in which nothing is discernable. "Up to that moment," says Carver, "Their life-history and conduct present nothing different from that of the lymph corpuscles."

But after that, all is changed. The granules that come into being in the clear field commence to act according to the law of a "new vitality," continues Carver, "and in such manner as to produce a new organism, composed primarily of the material brought from the parents of the gametes."

The Primary Cell appears as a tiny speck of transparent, structureless colloidal bioplasm. In this minute globule, a mysterious force, which appears to come form nowhere and which may be called Creative Intelligence, begins to perform peculiar work.

No eye can see the worker. No science has defined it. If examined under a microscope, nothing can be seen but the clear globule, which exhibits changes so fast, and yet so steady and purposeful if their succession, that they may be compared only with the work of an expert modeller upon a lump of soft clay.

The Silver Cord

This skillful process is not the work of what science calls "blind energy." It is the creative process of the mysterious Silver

Cord described by us in Pre-Existence of Man, Part II.

As with an invisible trowel, the globule is divided and subdivided into smaller particles, until it is reduced to an aggregation of specks small enough to build the finest fabric of the nascent organism.

It is then as if an invisible finger traced out the outline for the brain and spinal cord and proceeded to mold the contour of the body, fashioning flank and limb in due proportions so artistically that, after watching the work proceed hour by hour, one is possessed of the notion that some stronger aid to vision than an achromatic, would reveal the hidden artist with his blue-print before him striving with skillful manipulations to complete his task.

The invisible worker is the Silver Cord, the hidden artist, a stream of invisible electricity, the qualities and properties of which inhere in every part, particle, and electron in the Universe.

Keep these facts in mind as we proceed to describe the work performed by the cells, composed of atoms, which contain miniature solar systems that know what to do and how to do it.

Cosmic Radiation is a new term applied to highly penetrating forces travelling thru space at terrific speed and emanating from distant sources. As we have explained in Pre-Existence of Man, it is the most penetrating form of radiation known.

The rays are exceedingly rapid, charged with particles of electrons, protons, positrons, etc., which Dr. Millikan called the "birth cries of atoms."

This appears as the Transformative Principle in action. Men mention Creation as the beginning. There is no beginning. What we see and call Creation has always been in force and will always be. And what we see is only the visible presentation of Invisible Duplicates. In other words, what becomes visible must first exist in an invisible state.

Science recognizes and studies only the visible side of cosmic phenomena. The visible world and the visible man are merely the visible patterns of Invisible Duplicates, which exist as Four Primal Seed Atoms, as we have explained in Pre-Existence of Man.

Man was not created as the church teaches. He has existed always. We said the Primary Cell that begins the formation of man is the result of the male and female germinal elements. That Unit appears to constitute the Magic Cell which starts the formation of men.

When the gametes merged and fused, they seemed to disappear, leaving a clear field in which nothing appeared. Then, after a period of seeming quiescence, granulation began at the point between the places occupied by the gametes when they disappeared.

This granulated point in the beginning of the new person, and this point is the Four Seed Atoms carried by the Silver Cord. That is the Unit which constitutes the Magic Cell, the beginning of visible man.

The worker is Cosmic Radiation in the form of the Silver Cord. The blue- print before the worker is Pre-Existent Man, mentioned in the Bible as a building not made with hands, eternal in the heavens (1 Cor. 15:44; 2. Cor. 5:1).

Physical man is the visible replica of his Invisible Form which has existed always, and which comes into visible existence when the proper conditions are supplied.

For instance, clear light contains all the colors of the rainbow; but the colors do not become visible until certain conditions are supplied.

Invisible gases combine and appear as visible water under certain conditions. These gases also combine and appear as the Visible Man under certain conditions. That is Transformation, erroneously called Creation.

Visible things must first exist in an invisible state. Their appearance in the visible world depends on the occasion and condition which set into action the Process of Transformation.

Thousands of years ago the Accident Masters taught these things, but their literature has been destroyed by despots who know that ignorant people make peaceful slaves.

Paracelsus posited the theory of Cosmic Archetypes four hundred years ago, and this caused him to be driven from country to country by medical art and the church combined and was denounced as a fraud.

Prof. Lakhovsky recently presented the same theory in more scientific terms, which brought Plato's philosophy into harmony with scientific facts. His book is so revolutionary that it had a hard time to get into this country over the combined opposition of the church and medical art.

If we reject the postulate of man's pre-existence, as taught by the Ancient Masters, we must, to be consistent, admit his extinction at somatic death as asserted by modern science. For Solar Man cannot be eternal on one side and not be on the other.

Infinite Intelligence appears in the work of every cell, from the Primary Cell on thru the entire existence of the organism. By their inherent Intelligence, the cells know spontaneously the functions they are to perform in the construction and maintenance of the body. For that purpose, they are made.

Production is a process of division and subdivision from the Cosmic Circle down to infinitude. The law never changes. By dividing and subdividing the Cosmic Circle, out of its invisible essence all visible things appear, as if by magic. This productive process extends to infinitude in the Universe, down to the Primary Cell that builds the body.

Each body cell is a Circle, and each cell contains within itself the full potency of Productive Powers, as we shall see in the following illustration.

If we cultivate epithelial cells for a period of several months, entirely separate from the animal to which they belong, the cells automatically arrange themselves in a mosaic, exactly as though to protect a surface. Yet the surface they would protect is not there. But they carry out their purpose as though it were there.

The innate intelligence of the part the Cells play in the whole is a mode of being of all the elements of the Body. These elements know their work and can receive no aid from human hands.

* The Secret of Life.

Cells may be isolated, but they still possess the Productive Intelligence and Power of reproducing without apparent external direction or purpose, the structures characterizing each organism.

For instance, if some red blood corpuscles, impelled by gravity, flow from a drop of blood placed in liquid plasma and form a tiny stream, in a mysterious manner banks are soon built up; and these banks of cells just as mysteriously cover themselves with filaments of fibrin, forming a tube around the stream, thru which the corpuscles flow just as in a blood vessel, without the aid of a heart to "pump" them thru.

The medical theory of the heart's being a pump is just as preposterous as are all the other medical theories.

Next, in the same manner, the white blood-corpuscles appear, as if from nowhere. They adhere to the surface of the tube and surround it with their undulating membrane of cells.

The tube now assumes the form of a capillary blood vessel enveloped in a layer of contractile cells. It is the contraction and expansion of the cells, not the alleged pumping of the heart, that propels the blood on its way. Thus isolated, the red and white blood corpuscles construct out of cells a segment of the circulatory system, although there is no heart and no tissues to be irrigated.

More surprising, the body cells seem to understand numerology, geometry, physiology and biology and act concertedly for he interest of the whole. The spontaneous tendency toward the formation of the organs by their constitutive cells, in a primary datum of observation – but "medical science" cannot even attempt to offer any explanation of it.

Thus the body, from the Primary Cell on, is built by techniques and is directed by Intelligence that is entirely foreign to the best medical minds. It is absolutely not a process of blind physico-chemistry, as taught by "medical science."

For instance, an organ of the body is not made of visible, extraneous material, as is a house. It is made of invisible substance. Nor is it a cellular construction, a mere assemblage of cells; and yet, in a way, it is. For it is composed of cells, as a house is composed of bricks, but with this strange difference: The organ is born of and developed from one cell, a Primary Cell, as though a house originated from one brick---a magick brick that would immediately begin to make more bricks and do it without visible tools or visible material.

These bricks would come into being as if by magic and, without waiting for the architect's plan or the appearance of workers, would proceed to arrange themselves in regular order, as if by magic, and form the structure according to a definite plan. Stranger still, they would also metamorphose into window-glass, roofing-tile, casing boards, plaster, fuel for heating, water for kitchen and bathroom, etc.

This dumfounding work no man will ever understood. It cannot be explained. It is the mystery of the Great Intelligence.

As invisible atoms of dynamic force, the silver cord seemingly from out of nowhere, appears when and where needed, and the organs begin to develop in the embryo by a magic process such as that attributed to fairies in tales told children.

Truth is stranger than fiction, especially in this world of organized fraud and ignorance, where a Teacher of Truth is considered a dangerous person, because knowledge based on Truth sets man free from his enslavers (Jn. 8:32).

It should not be thought strange that the silver cord seems to appear out of nothing, when we know that all the colors of the rainbow just as seemingly appear out of nothing, being contained in the clear light surrounding the earth.

In that apparently clear light is contained all things that appear visible on earth. Simply supply the proper occasion and condition, and the forms appear on the visible plane.

From the Primary Cell composed of invisible atoms, and out of invisible substance contained in the clear light surrounding the earth, the body and its organs are produced by cells endowed with Infinite Intelligence.

It is astounding to observe that the cells by their work, prove that they possess a prevision of the future and its purpose, and they synthesize from the atomic substance that appears to be contained in the plasma, not only the building material, but also the builders.

The Eternal Elements of Universal Production are endowed with the properties of prevision and provision. They know the end from the beginning and the beginning from the end. These Elements proceed in an orderly cycle that has extended throughout all eternity. They know their purpose and their work. For they have always done it and will always do it as they are doing it now, eternally and forever.

As if by magic, the Primary Cell, by the productive process of division and subdivision, begins immediately to form more cells, without visible tools, without visible material, without food or drink. The additional cells appear out of nowhere as if by magic, and build the structure of the infant according to the eternal pattern that had no beginning. The cells also metamorphose into nails for fingers and toes, into hair for the head, eyebrows and eyelashes, into nerves and brain, into fluids for irrigation, into bones for the rigid framework, etc.

The molecules, atoms and electrons of which substance is composed are the Elements in different rates of vibration. They possess Infinite Intelligence direct from the Cosmic Source and know what to do and how to do it. They know where and how to unite and operate to form a leaf, a flower, a beast, a man. They need no doctor nor scientist to show them anything, and they perform their work properly and perfectly when not obstructed by the unnatural tactics and substances of the physicians, who claim they are aiding Nature in a task about which they know almost nothing at all.

The solarical forces are the Animating Principle. They interpenetrate all substance and, acting perpetually upon it, cause different rates of vibration in its different densities. The more subtle the substance, the less is the resistance to these forces and the higher the rate of vibration and the resulting consciousness.

THE MYTH OF NUTRITION

In an ancient prophecy of the Magi, it is foretold that "Man shall be blessed (in the regeneration –Mat. 19:28), no longer needing food."

The modern scientific theory of body nourishment is a myth.

The favorite abstraction of science, that the body cell is "a drop of gelatin surrounded by as semi-permeable membrane," is an illusion.

"Our ignorance (of the body's construction and function) is profound," wrote Dr. Carrel (Man, The Unknown, P. 4)

The modern world has no science of man. What passes as such is gross speculation.

The billions of cells forming the body are tiny suns and stars, composed of the same cosmic substance and governed by the same cosmic law.

A droplet of water forms a tiny microcosm containing, in a state of extreme dilution, a great variety of cosmic chemical elements. The body cell is practically a duplicate of a droplet of water, but raise to the high plane of divine animation.

Science shows that the cell is constituted of molecules, composed of atoms which are composed of electrons, and electrons are said to be whirling centers of force, endowed with eternalism. If that be true, as electrons eat no food, why should man?

The Primary Cell, not food, begins the building of the form of man. His body and organs are not built of food, but of cells produced by the division and subdivision of the trillions of cells that all come from that one Primary Cell. By the division of the pre-existing cells into two equal parts, the cells increase in number, and every part possesses similar properties.

Each cell has a definite life-history. It develops, performs its allotted work, and ceases to exist (1) either by dividing to form two new cells, or (2) by disintegrating and leaving the body as waste, being eliminated as gases and fluids. The cell-waste never leaves the body thru the bowels as feces.

The process of cell division is rapid in growing children, to supply the cells necessary to enable the organism to develop. Growth stops at maturity because the process of cell division decreases.

Then comes the time when the effects of bad environment and bad habits sooner or later begin to appear, and decay sets in, with somatic dissolution as the end of the body.

Physical science says that is the end of man. He is only a material form; and when the form ceases its function, his end has come.

If the cells depend on food and drink, as physical science claims, man should continue to grow and live as long as he had sufficient food and drink.

The vitality of the organism depends not on food and drink, for experience teaches athletes to go into action with empty stomachs.

That fact opened the eyes of Dr. Dewey and prompted him to write: "From the morning of medical history, the question of how vital energy is supported in time of sickness has never been considered, for there has never been any doubt in the medical mind as to that support coming from food (p. 40).

Physiologists find in tests on animals that feasting is more dangerous than fasting. They found that life lengthens when animals are subjected to certain periods of fasting. By the process of fasting and a frugal diet, they kept alive for three years worms that die in three or four weeks when well fed.

Professor Huxley, son of the elder Huxley, fed a family of earth worms as they usually eat, except one, which he isolated and fed the same way, but occasionally fasted it. That worm, alternately fed and fasted, was alive and vigorous after nineteen generations of its relatives had been born, lived their regular time, and died. He sought to explain the secret by saying that heavy eating clogs the life channels and so hastens death.

Applying Huxley's rule to man with similar results, instead of his dying at 100 and his friends thinking he had lived long, he would live almost 2,000 years. But "medical science" regards as fabulous the biblical account that Methuselah lived 969 years.

In his book, *Man The Unknown,* Carrel wrote:

"In primitive life, when men were healthy and lived long, they were subjected to long periods of fasting. When want did not compel them to fast, they voluntarily deprived themselves of food. All religions have insisted on the necessity of fasting. Fasting purifies and profoundly modifies and improves our tissues (p. 229).

"Life lengthens if animals are subject to fasting during certain fixed periods. Man's longevity could probably be increased by analogous or other procedures. (p.180).

"Life shortens because the body cells are not completely freed of waste products by the bloodstream. If the volume of the body fluids were much greater, and the elimination of waste products more complete, human life would last longer." (p.180)

The answer to these apparent defects is to eat less and drink more. Frequent feeding fills the body with dangerous waste products. Frugal feeding reduces them, and drinking freely helps the body to eliminate them. The fluid one drinks should be pure rain water and fruit juices.

We can train ourselves to do with less food. Adaptation of animals to hunger is easily noticeable. The cattle on the Arizona desert live healthy and long on far less food than those in lush pastures.

And, vice versa, we can move easily train ourselves to require more food than the body can use. By frequent eating and eating to excess, we develop habit hunger, a bad condition that clogs the body with waste and hastens death.

In his "Believe It Or Not, "Ripley said that Gilman Lowe, weight lifter and health director, after fasting for three weeks, mounted a scale adjusted to 1000 pounds net. The scale was equipped with a steel platform, against which Lowe braced his back. He braced and lifted 1,006 times in succession, until each time the scale registered half a ton—a total of 1,006,000 pounds, in 34 minutes and 35 seconds (New York—1903). Lowe was the holder of 35 world's records for endurance lifting.

The press of April 3, 1934, contained a picture of August Gearing, age 60, who had just finished a 44 day fast. He said, "It's grand feeling and a wonderful aid to health to fast. I feel better every time I fast. My motto is: Take an occasional fast; eat to live, and live long. We add years to our life-span with every fast."

John W. Armstrong of London reported to us in 1933 the case of a patient who began to fast under his supervision October 31, 1932, and fasted 100 days and 6 hours, taking nothing but water. Doctors could do nothing for the victim, and fasting was suggested by a Naturist as a lost hope. The man not only regained health, but his face appeared "twenty years younger" wrote Armstrong when his body was built up after the fast.

Dr. Carlson and Kunde, University of Chicago, found that a fast of 15 day restored the tissues of a man of 40 to the physiological condition of those of a youth of 17. This fact seems to explain the biblical statement, "His flesh shall be fresh as a child's; he shall return to the days of his youth (Job 33:25). And thy youth shall be renewed like eagle's" (Ps. 103:5).

The press in 1931 reported that Mrs. Albert G. Walker, a noted singer of South Africa, fasted 101 days, taking nothing but water. She weighed 232 pounds when the fast began and 169 pounds when it ended. She want to parties, carried on her public singing, and was in good health at the end of her fast, the report said.

In his "Believe It Or Not, "in the press of January 16,1934, Ripley stated that Jekisiel Laib, of Grodno, Poland, fasted six days a week for 30 years. Each Saturday he ate bread and water. His health was good.

This is proof that dietetic experts don't know their subject. It shows they are all wrong in their theory that man must eat this for protein, that for mineral salts, something else for vitamins, and so on. In a word, they know nothing about diet.

In his "Believe It Or Not," in the press of January 25, 1938, Ripley stated that for ten years Giovanni Succi travelled thru Europe giving exhibitions of fasting. His exhibitions, rigidly controlled, extended for periods of 30 40 days. During that time, he was in the public eye day and night. Included were 80 periods of 30 days of fasting, and 20 periods of 40 days of fasting a total of 3200 days without eating, or eight years and 280 days without eating in ten yours.

The press of November 30, 1934, reported the case of a Jain priest, Muni Shri Misrilaiji, of Bombay, who fasted for 259 days, taking nothing but water. This East Indian Priest ended his fast in the presence of 500 co-religionists.

The press of October 12, 1948, reported the case of a British girl of 12 years who fasted for 18 months, taking nothing but water.

The press of February 6, 1937, quoted Mrs. Martha Nasch, age 44, of St. Paul, Minnesota, as asserting that for seven years she had eaten nothing and affirmed her willingness to submit to surveillance to prove her claim.

The press of May 31, 1948, reported the case of a Chinese girl who had eaten nothing for nine years.

The case was reported by Dr. T. Y. Gan, of Chungking Municipal Hospital, who heard of the girl and went to see her. He said her name was Yang Mei, that she was 20 years old, weighed about 85 pounds, and led a perfectly normal life, except for not eating and drinking very little water.

She showed no signs of starvation and appeared no different from other girls. Gan said, "I found it difficult to believe her story."

The girl had no desire for food, and never asked for any. When questioned as to why she did not drink more, she said that it made her feel uncomfortable.

The press of London, of October 16, 1949, stated that Teresa Neuman, a German peasant mystic, had eaten no solid food for 14 years. It was also claimed that not a drop of liquid has passed her lips for 10 years. And she had been without sleep all the time.

In an article entitled, "Forty years Without Food," N. P. Ghose wrote:

"Garibala Dassi, sister of Babu Lamboxar Dey, a practicing pleader of Purulia, has been living for the last forty years without taking any food, not even water, and has been doing her regular household duties with no apparent injury to her health. Many respectable persons can testify to the truth of this statement. "— India's Message, January 1932.

According to the press of May 27, 1937, Sirmati Bala, of Bankura, India, age 68, had touched no food nor water since she was 12 years old.

In 1949 we received a report from a lady in England who said she had discovered how to grow young. Her secret is to dispense with all food. She has lived for years on liquids and takes nothing for two months at a time while climbing mountain for exercise.

It is her opinion that the whole food problem is an illusion. She believes that she gets direct from the air and sunshine all the minerals her body needs.

One case is enough to prove what is possible in a million other cases. Biologists are being convinced that eating is an acquired habit and a pleasurable indulgence rather that a physiological necessity. It is said that in India certain sects of yogis live without eating and that in the Himalayas there are many who consume no physical food.

"An organ (the structures of the body) builds itself by techniques very foreign to the human mind. It is not made of extraneous material, like a house," (Carrel, in Man, The Unknown, p. 107).

According to modern science, the body and its organs are built and maintained by what man eats and drinks. Carrel opposes that theory. He says that the body and its organs are not made of "extraneous material,"

Carrel continues: "It (the organ) is composed of cells, as a house is composed of bricks. But he organ is born from a cell, as if the house originated from one brick—a magic brick that would set about manufacturing more bricks," (P. 108).

Carrel shows that all organs and structures of the body come from the Parent Cell. The subsequent cells come from the division of the Parent Cell and the subdivision of the resultant cells.

The Parent Cell and the Cells that come from the Parent Cell are "hot made of extraneous material, like a house," says

Carrel. He means that the cells are not composed of what man eats and drinks.

We saw that the body begins at the point where two tiny cells fuse, which forms what we term the Parent Cell, the positive and negative poles. And at this point the Pour Seed Atoms appear, as if by magic, in the Silver Cord, as described in Part II of *Pre-Existence of Man.*

The Parent Cell is not the product of food, nor is it sustained by food. What food does not and cannot produce it cannot and does not sustain.

The growth of the body does not result from food consumption, but from the division and subdivision of the Parent Cell. The cells are composed of molecules which are composed of atoms which are composed of electrons whirling at terrific speed.

It is difficult to realize that the electrons in the atoms which constitute the cells of the body whirl at such high speed that it requires nine feet of solid lead to slow down one electron to where photograph of it can be taken.

The force of the electron is the force of the atom, which is the force of the cells, which is the force of the body. There are approximately 42 trillions of cells in the average human body, each composed of electrons whirling at lightning speed.

These and other discoveries constrained Carrel to throw up his hands in despair and confess: --

"The science of man is still too rudimentary to be useful. The illusions of the mechanists of the 19th century, (and) the childish physico-chemical conceptions of the human being have to be definitely abandoned." (Man, The Unknown, P. 108, 179).

That unqualified declaration of this great doctor upsets every theory contained in medical text-book, every dogma of medical art, every precept of medical practice, and every assumption as to the cause and care of human ailments. It shatters the claims concerning energy, food and feeding advanced by "dietetic experts," It indicates that almost nothing is known about the nutritive demands of the organism and how to supply them.

Practically everything taught in modern times as to these and related subjects is erroneous and even dangerous, and should be "definitely abandoned" according to the impartial findings of Carrel, who spent his life attempting to solve the mystery of Man, and who showed that living cells are immortal by keeping the fragments of a chicken's heart alive for 27 years it was removed from the body.

The body appears as a material form. But that material does not enter the body as food and water. That material is condensed substance, as water and ice are condensed invisible substance.

Man's body is not built of material substance, such as food and water, nor by a mechanical or physico-chemical process as claimed by physical science.

The body is composed and constituted of invisible substance, produced and maintained by a cosmic process of condensation, materialization and transformation.

The body is the product of electrons, atoms and molecules, which build the cells which build the body. These building blocks, as Millikan calls them, are not produced nor sustained by food.

The vital processes of the body cannot be traced to their ultimate origin, except in the Mind. Attempts to do so lead to a point of irresistible opposition to further analysis.

Occult science takes up the metaphysical thread at this point and traces its course into the Indivisible Realm, guided by the Mind and the philosophy of the Master, that "the invisible things from the creation of the world are clearly seen (in the mind), being understood by the things made (visible)." – Rom. 1:20.

The formation of cells within the body is constantly occurring from birth to death. There is no evidence to show that what one eats and drinks enters into the cell formation. That is what Carrel asserts. He says that the cells are not made of "extraneous materials."

The physiologist shows that there passes from the body, thru the bowels, kidneys, lungs and skin, the exact amount of liquids and solids that man consumes in eating and drinking.

Stone and metal, in gaseous and invisible form, float in the air. So do wood and coal. Also flesh and bone. Yes, everything known to man.

No chemist can find in the ground in which grows a giant tree, the ash, minerals, carbon, wood and chlorophyll contained in the tree and its leaves.

Neither does the tree consume the soil in which it stands. If so, then as evidence of such consumption a depression should surround every tree.

As sunshine, air, soil and water do nothing more than stimulate the inherent functions innate in the cells of the tree, so what man consumes does nothing more than help to stimulate the cells of his body into their requisite functions.

Cell and body nutrition is a myth. What man consumes does not supply cell nutrition by assimilation as taught by science. The ingested substances produce activity in cell function by stimulation.

Two types of stimulation seem essential for the function of living cells:

(1) vital and (2) chemical. The nerves of the body supply the vital, and food and liquid supply the chemical.

The free flow of nerve force to all pats of the body is the first requisite to normal function, as proven by the science of chiropractic. This is had by fasting, and explains why fasting is so effective in building health in sick bodies.

With normal nerve stimulation, the body can exist for weeks without food consumption. Nor are any certain kinds of food necessary, except that unheated and uncooked substances supply a more natural quality of chemical stimulation than heated and cooked substances.

The elements of the food contact and stimulate the body cells into action, and pass out of the body thru the eliminative channels, as flowing water turns the wheel of a mill on the bank of the stream, and thus activates the machinery in the mill that does the grinding.

A profound mystery the work of the mill would be to him who knew not the secret of the water-wheel.

As long as normal nerve force reaches the various organs, the cells of the organs respond properly to the particular food stimuli that activate them. If for any reason the nerve force is weak, that weakens the cells; and they loss their power to react properly to food stimulants.

The result is illness which doctors treat. If patients recover under the doctor's care, it is in spite of his treatment and not because of it.

Biochemists show that a plant possesses a laboratory that transforms invisible substance of the air into cell material. The cells of the leaf split the water molecules of the air into oxygen and hydrogen, rejecting the oxygen atoms and appropriating the hydrogen atoms for replacement cells.

AIR CHANGED TO WOOD

The press of January 3, 1954, reported that Dr. Paul M. Laughton and Dr. D.C. Mortimer, two members of the Canadian National Research Council, showed by test that the leaves of sugar beets changed air into solid wood in 10 seconds.

The leaves were exposed to small amounts of carbon dioxide gas under a bright light. The gas was first made radioactive so it could be identified when it got inside the plant. The leaves were allowed to absorb the gas for varying periods and then were killed in boiling water.

Radioactive cellulose was found in the leaves even though they had absorbed the gas ONLY 10 seconds.

In view of these scientific findings, it is logical to assume that the body's laboratory is competent to change air into blood, bone and flesh.

The experiments of Richards showed that in the plant's laboratory the disintegration of acids thru the division of the acid compounds is not a digestive but a respiratory process, and results from the alternative oxidation and de-oxidation of the plant tissues thru the action of cosmic radiation. He held that the same principle applies to man to a certain extent.

It would be absurd to suggest that the human body is less efficiently equipped to care for its needs than is the lowly weed.

The Masters said, "Every Element nourishes itself." This applies to electrons, atoms and molecules—the units of which liquids and solids are composed.

Modern science boasts the fact that it has finally advanced to the primary stage of condensing or materializing air. The spider, hornet and wasp have always performed that miracle without the necessity of attending a human school of chemistry.

The modus operandi by which the laboratory of these animals condenses web and paper from the air they inhale is the despair of science. The laboratory of these animals also condenses from the air the substance needed to sustain their bodies.

Biochemists assert that the function of the intestinal tract is to serve as a laboratory for condensing and combining nascent hydrogen gas with nitrogen gas entering the lungs as air. They regard the lungs, not the stomach, as the chief organs of digestion, with the intestinal tract serving only to carry on its primary function of condensing, combining and eliminating.

Biologists hold that oxygen gas supports the cells and that nitrogen gas acts as a tissue builder and vitalizer. Nitrogen is found in the muscles and fibrous tissues and is said to be the first of all the elements to leave the dead body. Then tissue decomposition begins.

Physiologists declare that without hydrogen creative activity in the body would cease. There would be no elimination, no perspiration, no salivation.

Hydrogen is needed in the blood and cells. It soothes the nerves, regulates body temperature, moistens lung surface, carries off toxins, cools the tissues and retards inflammation. Without hydrogen, the nerves and tissues would stiffen, harden and decay.

Harold W. Percival, in his great work titled, Thinking and Destiny, describes various changes which occur in the body when man no longer eats as he does now. He said:

"The blood gradually ceases to build to build and maintain the body. It acts more as a conveyer of nerve force... Nutrition is taken in by the breath directly from the four stages of matter. The brain takes and sends impressions more easily than was possible before. The spinal cord assumes more and more the appearance of brain structure. Its central canal becomes larger, and the terminal filament, which is now atrophied from disuse, is greatly enlarged. Its central canal, which at present is threadlike and is lost on its way to the end of the filament, is widened and reaches to the very tip of the filament. The intestinal tract ceases to be a feeding tube and a sewer, and the anus disappears. The stomach and small intestines are then superfluous and disappear.

"The large bowel or colon, then serving a new purpose, becomes part of a nerve structure, similar to the spinal cord, termed the front-or-nature-cord. This cord with its lateral branches is made up of the former esophagus, of the two cords and the plexuses and the increased ramification of the involuntary nerve system, and of the colon. The middle of the three bands that extend along the exterior wall of the colon, become hollowed out, and around this canal is arranged the colon, greatly reduced in size, so that only a short, narrow tubular cord remains, as part of the front-cord.

"Included in the front-cord are the right and left vagus nerves, with their ramifications. It is situated in front of the abdominal cavity and is curved from before backward, pointing toward the tip of the terminal filament of the voluntary nerve system.

"The front-cord becomes enclosed in a resilient structure, here termed the front- or nature-cord. This replaces the sternum and is extended to and is continuous with the greatly changed pelvic bowl. The body is thus a two-columned organism...

"There are other changes in the body in addition to those given, which will obtain when the human enters the Life Path. Nerves not now visible will become active and will affect chiefly the lungs and heart. The lungs will then become active like the cerebrum, and, and the heart with the aorta, the thymus and other glands, like the cerebellum and pons,--pp. 720-722.

Biochemists come close to an old truth when they assert that "food does not form the organic part of the blood, but supplies only the mineral base by setting free the cell-salts contained in foods."

We have on file a record of the case of one Professor Marshall, who fell ill while working alone in the South American jungles, and was found and attended by "uncivilized" Indians. He became unconscious and so remained for seven months, during which time he ate and drank nothing.

The Indians treated him in their usual way of caring for the sick, by anointing his body all thru the period of his unconsciousness. When he recovered consciousness, he was not only well, but had gained in weight.

Physical science declares that the human body is animated, vitalized, nourished and maintained by the material food eaten, digested, and assimilated by the body cells thru a direct chemical process.

No orthodox scientist dares question that theory, and no scientist ever lived who could analyze and explain the process in an intelligent and logical manner, because that alleged process is purely imaginary.

The body is built and composed of cells. We trace back thru the cells, molecules and atoms to the electrons, which are said to be whirling centers of force in the other.

In the Mind, we say reverse the process and see that invisible substance condensing, from invisible electrons, atoms and molecules, into visible elements, forms and entities, by a natural condensing process resulting from retardation of the vibrations.

It is common knowledge that invisible gases condense to form water and ice. It should be as easy to understand that, under the same law, these invisible gases condense to form blood, flesh, bones, and the entire body--according to a pre-existent pattern, as declared by the Masters:

"We have a building, a house not made with hands, eternal in the heavens," (2 Cor. 5:1).

The Bible tells a surprising story when its parables and allegories are understood and are divorced from the preposterous interpretations of theology.

Splitting the atom proves that there is a mighty force inherent in invisible substance which condenses and forms visible Matter. Its modus operandi never alters, and it acts constantly on man, in his cells, thru his cells, operating simultaneously on all planes of being-yet appearing not to manifest itself in concrete form.

The Force, under the control of Infinites Intelligence, possesses the property of activating and stimulating atoms to assume various relationship according to law and galvanizes the power latent in dormant cells into a higher state of activity.

It is said that in man's present degenerate state, food is one of the essential medium thru which this force acts in his organism. In the early days, before man had suffered degeneration, even this medium was not necessary.

"How can we prevent the degeneracy of man in modem civilization?" asks Carrel in despair. (P. 5).

The Masters held that the Four Cosmic Elements of fire, air, water, and earth are the builders, substainers and regenerators of the body. These are the four phases of the Cosmic Ray, as follows, Thermic, Atmospheric, Fluviatic and Terrestrial.

These four rays are charged with all the elements of the living organism and many more. The four major elements are said to be nitrogen, oxygen, hydrogen and carbon.

In these days of organized fraud, deception and darkness, the subject of nutrition is little understood. It is ruled by a force outside of thought or will.

It appears that in his present degenerate state, man must depend on food because he has lost the primary consciousness of the law governing the force that impairs action to all parts of the body. There is a law that rules the action of the constantly flowing stream or regenerative current directed upon Matter.

Occult science holds that when man, by regeneration, again becomes conscious of this law, he will be able to assimilate this force, and no longer be dependent upon gross matter (food) to aid in the support of his organism.

Abbe N. De Montfaucon De Villars states in his book that the Ancient Masters ate food only for pleasure and never necessity (*compte De Gabalis*, P. 63).

Paracelsus himself says that he lived for six months without eating. He received his sustaining elements from the "particles of dynamic spirit, the Ray of Invisible Substance, entering the lungs from the air."

Because of his startling work, and for attacking their false theories and definitions, and for "curing" by unorthodox methods the patients for whom the orthodox doctors could do nothing, they hired thugs to kill him by throwing him over a cliff.

Ehret reports cases of religious devotees who have fasted for decades. He held that the purer the body, the less it needs food. When the body is perfectly pure and in normal condition, the need for food practically vanishes. When there are impurities still in the body, acids form in the fluids, creating a need for alkalies in the form of fruits and vegetables, which supply the body with activity in ell function by stimulation.

When one eats salty and seasoned food, this causes unnatural thirst that disappears when one eats uncooked and unseasoned food consisting of green vegetables, tomatoes, melons, berries and fruits. The sale and seasoning substances irritate he cells, and they cry for help in the form of fluid to dilute and wash away the irritants.

Starchy substances absorb so much fluid from the cells, that the cells are forced to call for more fluid.

Cell irritation by the acid-forming substances man eats, causes the cells to call for fluid to neutralize the toxins creating the irritation.

Grains, cereals and tubers, unnatural substances produced by strenuous toil, form the major portion of the modern diet in he cold zone. These substances consist chiefly of starch, which cannot be utilized by the body until it becomes soluble and usable by a chemical change that converts the starch into dextrine and then into glucose.

It is just as simple to create an unnatural demand for food as for water.

Each kind of food at a meal creates new hunger by chemical stimulation. The mono-diet system reduces the demand for food by reducing stimulation.

At a meal one eats baked beans until hunger is satisfied. New hunger may then be produced by eating bread and butter. Follow that with pie, and more hunger appears. Additional hunger will appear when the ice-cream and cake are served.

This is due to the fact that each kind of food produces its own type of stimulation that appears in the sensation of hunger.

This leaves the fatal opening for the dietetic expert. He tells his victims that such method of eating fails to furnish the body with all the various elements it needs. And so it goes; the blind leading the blind, and they all fall in the ditch. (Mat. 15:14).

Unnatural thirst and unnatural hunger are produced by stimulation and irritation. Our sensations of thirst and hunger are largely unnatural and abnormal—the result of an unnatural mode of living that become normal in theory because so prevalent in practice.

Raise your voice against this or any form of conventionalism, and you are a fanatic because you stand alone—as did Columbus when he declared the earth is round.

Standing alone on a theory is not evidence per se that you are wrong. But that evidence is too strong against you and too weak to win many converts. One feels safer to follow the multitude than to follow the lone disciple of grace and godliness.

The culinary art, the practice of food preparation and cookery, has transformed man from a god to a glutton.

According to Evans, man has no need to eat protein. There is physiological proof that man inhales nitrogen directly from the air; and, by the union of carbon compounds with ammonia, formed by the combination of nitrogen from the air with the nascent hydrogen in the intestines, protein is synthetically formed in the body's laboratory.

As for fats and carbohydrates, on these the body does not depend for heat and energy as physical science claim. They are a liability to the body, not as asset.

If man does not eat acid-forming substances, minerals are not lost by the body to any marked extent, and the small replacement required comes from the air.

It appears that another need for food is to supply alkalies to neutralize the acid toxins produced by the consumption of acid-forming foods.

Crile asserted that death occurs at the moment when positive acidity is established in the organism. He showed that "all inhalation anesthetics cause a progressively increased hydrogen ion concentration, with death occurring at the moment when a positive acidity is established."

The acid-alkali balance of the body has a vital significance. When the alkalinity of the blood falls, the animal dies. This balance between the nucleus and the cytoplasm of the cells (the electric potential), is essential to animation and supplies the vitality of the living process itself. Its reduction to equilibrium (neutrality) or zero, produces death.

The cytoplasm of the cell surrounding the nucleus is the negative (alkaline) element. The nucleus is the positive (acid) element. The nucleus represents the positive pole and the cytoplasm, the negative pole. This makes the cell a bipolar mechanism, a fact referred to in our work titled Pre-Existence of Man.

As a result of the oxidation of the lipoid films (oily membrane), acids are produced, with a resultant increase in the hydrogen ion concentration and an increased potential in the cell membrane

The essential characteristics of vitality manifested in the cells as assimilation, growth and generation, depend not upon food, but upon the presence of an electric potential that is produced by oxidation, says Crile. The various functions of the organs are due to a variation of the potentials.

Hydrogen is an acid, and hydrogen ions (positive charged particles) permeate all living organisms. The slightest charges in the hydrogen ion concentration fundamentally alters the organism, and hydrogen ions are of high electrical significance.

The primary steps on the path to regeneration are a return to man's natural habitat in the zone of eternal spring, pure outside air always, vegetarianism, uncooked and unseasoned food, the mono-diet regimen, and rigid conservation of the life fluid. The vital essence that produces new life will preserve the old life if not expended.

Jeans writes that "Cosmic rays break up millions of atoms in the body every second, and the physiological effect is the vitality of the organism."

By means of atomic action termed fire, a fluid called gasoline is converted into a force that propels giant air-planes thru the air and carries man thru space at terrific speed.

Cosmic rays flow thru the unperceivable states of essence and become visible in the radiating and gaseous form, finally assuming the visible states of fluids and solids, or blood, bones and flesh.

Science shows that vegetables possess machinery which converts atmospheric elements into sustaining substance.

This fact proves that physical growth, generation and maintenance are not the gross physico-chemical processes claimed by physical science.

Certain advanced groups know even now that vitalization of the ductless glands may be increased by deeply breathing of pure outside air. This constitutes the basis of special training for those who embrace the task of better development of body and brain, termed Initiation.

The new knowledge we have as to the composition of Matter makes it more difficult to explain why man should eat than to show that he should never have to eat.

The paramount fact appears in every investigation –that man consumes much more food than he should for his good.

VEGETARIANISM IS BAD

"We eat to live, and we eat to die."— Charles W. De Lacy Evans, M.R.C.S.E., late surgeon to St. Saviour's Hospital, London, in his work, How to Prolong life, P. 28.

A puzzling paradox. If we eat to live, how can we eat to die? If we eat to die, how can we eat to live? That mystery we are now engaged in considering in this work.

The vegetarian thinks his diet puts him a big step ahead of the flesh cater; but the records show that the average health and the average life-span of the average Vegetarian are not above that of the average Carnivorian.

In his reference to Vegetarians, Dr. Evans wrote:

"Cereals and farinacous foods form the basis of the diet of the so-called 'vegetarians,' who are guided by no direct principle, except that they believe it is wrong to eat animal food. For this reason, vegetarians have no better health and live no longer than those around them." (Densmore, P. 303).

We shall be guided by a direct principle in this discussion and learn the reason why vegetarianism is bad, and why many continue to consume flesh in spite of the long campaign against the practice.

It is well to remember that the less vital the body is, the more poison it will endure without discomfortable reactions. When danger threatens and the body is too weak to defend itself, that man is in a serious state. Poison will not affect a dead man, and it affects a half-dead man less than it does a more vital man.

An example: As the killing cold dormantizes the peripheral nerves of the body, they become unable to convey danger signals to the brain, and the freezing man no longer notices the cold. In fact, he begins to feel warm; and then he becomes unconscious, feels nothing, and freezes to death.

Most adults know that tobacco and liquor are bad for the body. They are nerve and brain poisons. The use of these lowers the vitality; and the body, due to a reduction of its powers, adjusts itself physiological to their use.

BODY VITALITY REDUCED

The same principle applies to eating. When the Breatharian ate his first food, it affected his nerves adversely, just as the first smoke adversely affects the youth. But the youth persists until the poisonous tobacco dulls his nerves and lowers his vitality; and thus his body adjusts itself to the use of tobacco not only, but in time, comes to crave the poisonous weed.

So the Breatharian continues to eat in spite of the ill effect of it, with the result that the body's vitality was reduced because the brain and nerves were dulled. His body, thus weakened, adjusted itself to the unnatural, enervating practice of eating, and he began to crave food.

And it came to pass that as the substances the Breatharian ate weakened his body, man actually eats to die just as he smokes to die.

We must not miss the fact that he who eats has never had the amount of vitality that man's body originally possessed as a Breatharian. We refer not to physical strength, but to that physiological vitality which carries man on thru the years and keeps him as nimble at ninety as he was at thirty. For the turning of the earth on its axis has o affect on the body.

We must understand that the process of vital adjustment necessary for the body to tolerate a substance it is not made to receive internally is actually one of vital reduction.

The enervated body will endure without protest a dangerous enemy which the vital body wars against and strives to subdue and eliminate. The symptoms of that struggle are termed disease by the doctors.

It took time to modify and weaken the body so that it would not only tolerate, but crave, the poisonous plants and herbs, termed vegetables, which constitute the diet of the vegetation.

MOST VEGETABLES ARE NOT NATURAL

Most of the vegetables man eats are not found growing wild in Nature. The fields in which they grow are man-made.

God made no mistake when he covered the earth with trees. The science of forestry shows that deforestation lays the land open and naked to the fury of the wind, the scorching rays of the sun, and to erosion and destructive floods.

Authorities on the subject assert that many waste regions and deserts were once teeming with fertility and foliage; and the existing sterility of these places in the work of man in the destruction of forests.

Man's burdens rise from his foolish efforts to modernize the Primitive and artificialize the Natural. Striking examples of the catastrophes that result from this work are the deserted Dust Bowls of the earth.

Fields are artificial; annual crops are artificial; their cultivation is artificial.

Fields are work of man in his effort to "improve" on Nature. The cultivation of these fields is as artificial as the fields are as artificial as their cultivation.

All forms of artificialization disturb the equilibrium of Nature, and the result are always disastrous, says Professor John C. Gifford, University of Miami, Florida, who wrote:

"Fields are sun-baked in dry weather and muddy and eroded in the rain season, where cultivation is entirely artificial, and where the equilibrium of Nature has been completely upset by the work of man. All these cultivated things would die and disappear without the pampering hand of man." (Tropical Subsistence Homestead, P. 95).

The Vegetarian has grown vain in his conceit. He has discarded animal products and feels that he has found dietetic perfection in vegetables, grains, cereals, legumes and tubers. Scientific investigation and his own deficient physical and mental condition prove that he is no better off than his flesh-eating friends.

Unbiased investigation shows that the modern Vegetarian is travelling the wrong trail. The things he eats are not natural products, nor the natural food of man. They are definitely artificial.

1. Grains and cereals have been developed from insignificant grass seeds. By long ages of seed selection, careful breading, intensive cultivation and constant fertilization, small grass seeds were developed by this artificial process into the modern grains and cereals.
2. Beans, peas, lentils, cabbage, lettuce, celery, etc., were developed in the same way from the grass family.
3. Tubers, which include potatoes, onions, carrots, turnips, beets, radishes, etc., are nothing more than wild weed roots, developed by

the artificial process above described.

Years ago Knight, in his "Vegetable Food of Man," asserted that grains and cereals have been developed from insignificant grass seeds now unknown to botany. Dir. Ernest Densmore, in his Natural Food of Man, wrote:

"Grains are the product of the temperate zone, not of those regions where there is no winter; and it was therefore a necessity of man's sustenance when he was without agriculture, without tools, and without fire, and had to depend upon foods spontaneously produced by Nature, that he live in a region where foods were produced at all seasons of the year. This narrows of confines the inquiry of natural food to two articles—fruits and nuts." (p. 224).

Vegetarians hate to hear their diet criticized, and most of them refuse to read or believe anything that is not favorable to vegetarianism.

C.C. Hibba, D.D.S., wrote an excellent article on Dental Decay, in which he said:

"Grains are responsible for nearly all of men's disease, for wheat, barley, oats and rye are no more a part of his food than oranges the food of the cow, or grains the food of dogs and cats.

‘Man’s food consists of the frits and nuts of the tree. They are beautifully wrapped and hung on trees where the common herd cannot get to them. Man is given hands with which to remove his food and its wrappings, and eat to his content and perfect health.

“Eliminate grains from man’s food and the decay in children’s teeth will cease. Tarter and pyorrhea will disappear. The hospitals will fold up, and medicine will be a dream. All the doctors on earth and their ‘vast’ medical experience cannot disprove this statement.

“The medical profession dare not take a group of children and feed them according to Nature’s law for a period of six months, and then truly publish the results.” (You can’t Eat That.)

CEREALS ARE A BAD FOOD

A German physician of note, Dr. Winckler, after enthusiastically adopting a vegetarian diet, was horrified to find in time that his blood vessels showed signs of cretaceous degeneration. With natural solicitude, he applied himself to a solution of the phenomenon.

He said he found the explanation in a work by Dr. Monin, of Paris, who, in turn, had been directed to the exploration of atheroma (arteriosclerosis, hardening of the arteries) by Professor Gubler of Paris.

The substance of the explanation was that the mineral salts in the vegetables and the salt and seasonings used on the vegetables to make them palatable are bad not only for their early effect on the body, but also because they induce the desire for, and the practice of, taking other and stronger stimulants.

In our work, SCIENTIFIC LIVING, we mentioned the case of Captain Diamond who, as a vegetarian for 30 years, proved on himself that vegetables are not the panacea they are believed by many to be. His diet as a vegetarian consisted of grains, cereal products, tubers and green vegetables. At 79 he was a chronic invalid, suffering from a serious state of hardened tissues and blood-vessels, with stiffness of the joints.

The muscles of his legs and back were so stiff that he could not sit down nor rise from a chair without great discomfort, and he often needed the aid of an assistant. The tissues of his hand and arms were so stiff that it was hard for him to hold his knife and work to feed himself.

Orthodox doctors were unable to help him and pronounced him incurable. They told him that he could not live long. He turned to Nature, became a fruitarian, and recovered health sufficiently to outlive all the doctors who gave him up, dying at the age of 120.

Diamond's and other cases of vegetarians supply data showing that vegetarianism is not what it is supposed to be. Grains and tubers contain large quantities of mineral salts that harden and stiffen the tissues, blood-vessels and joints, "and as a class," writes Densmore, "are the worst adapted as food for man."

Dr. Rowbotham adduced proof in his work published in 1841, showing that "cereal foods tend to ossification (hardening) of tissues and joints, and produce decrepitude and early death." (*Natural food of man,* P. 390).

FRUITS EASIER PRODUCED WITH LESS LABOR

Dr. G. Monin of Paris, wrote:

"A vegetable diet ruins the blood-vessels and makes one prematurely old, if it be true that man is as old as his arteries." (p. 312).

All authorities, both sacred and profane, agree that man was a frugivorian before he became a vegetarian. They also show that not only are fruits easier produced with less labor, but that any given portion of land is capable of producing more human food, with less labor, in the form of fruit, than under any other mode of culture.

Down thru the ages the body has been forced to adjust itself to everything man eats. Every herb of the field contains substances that are poisonous to him who has never eaten them. Not poisonous enough generally to kill him instantly, but often poisonous enough to make him sick even now, after having eaten them for thousands of years.

Certain foods still give some people diarrhea, yet they have eaten them all their days. To do that they must be poisonous to the body.

Green corn, roasting ears, often give people loose bowels. Strawberries, tropical mangoes, and other substances often cause a rash on the skin.

The fluid from the stem-end of a mango will poison some people as poison ivy will. If the wind blows thru the damp foliage of a mango tree unto the face of some folks for a sufficient length of time. Their face will swell until their eyes are almost closed. A child of tree years recently suffered from skin rash on much of its body from handling mangoes and not eating them. The mango is considered one of the finest of tropical fruits.

When foods cause skin rash, some doctors order the eating of them stopped, while others say the rash is the result of a purging process that the body needs. The rash is similar to that of ivy poisoning, so why not be consistent and hold that the rash of ivy poisoning is the result of a purging process?

Vegetarians who read this will wonder what to eat. Melons contain no poisonous elements and much distilled fluid that is good for the body. Tomatoes are not so good, but are better than many other vegetables because of their large liquid content.

Man should return to berries and fruits and become a frugivorian, and than to fruit juices as he progresses toward Breatharianism by constantly reducing food consumption and dissipating the hunger sensation.

The press recently reported the cases of man who has been unconscious for four years as the result of a car accident. During this time, the nurse gave him a liquid diet. For that time he was a liquidarian.

Could man perform what is termed manual labor on such diet? What we call manual labor is unnatural. Wild animals do not engage in it. God did not intend man should chop wood all day, shovel coal or dig potatoes or post holes, and come in at night so tired he can hardly drag one foot after the other. Such labor is not natural and is degenerating.

Spencer said that Perfect Correspondence must prevail. One thing calls for another to balance it. We must apply the law of correspondence to everything.

In that word "Adaptability," lies the secret of degeneration and regeneration, advancement and retrogression. The law of vital Adjustment makes man correspond always with his work, his habits, and his environment.

Adaptability is the quality that makes this possible. Man's existence depends on the flexibility, pliability and adaptability of his body in order that it may be able to accommodate itself to new and varying condition.

The state of Correspondence brings into operation the process of Vital Adjustment, and the purpose is to make man's body harmonize with his habits, his work, and his environment. These things become simple when the basic principle is understood.

ALIMENTATION AND DECREPTITUDE

Parallax in his "Patriarchial Longeviity," Easton and Bailey in their "Records of Longevity, "Hufeland in his "Art of Prolonging Life," and Evans in his "How to Prolong Life," all substantially agree that the CAUSE of decrepitude called Old Age, is not the work of Time, but the result of ossification and the deposition of calcareous earthy matter in the body-and it comes from what man eats, drinks and breathes.

What are the causes of the difference between youth and old age? Why do the functions of the body weaken and the organs deteriorate? Why does man become decrepit and die?

In Old Age there is a furious, gelatinous and earthy deposit in the body. The solid earthy matter which, by gradual accumulation in the body, brings on ossification, rigidity, decrepitude and death, is composed chiefly of phosphate of lime, carbonate of lime (common chalk), and sulphate of lime (plaster paris), with magnesia and traces of other earthy substances.

A process of solidification begins as soon as the infant begins to eat and continues without interruption until the body is changed from a comparatively fluid, elastic, and energetic state, to a solid, earthy, rigid, weakened condition, which terminates in death.

Infancy, childhood, youth, manhood and decrepitude are so many different conditions of the body or stages in the process of solidification or ossification. The only difference in the body between youth and Old Age is the greater density and rigidity, and the greater proportion of calcareous earthy matter that enter into its composition.

EARTH SALTS CAUSE OLD AGE

Common table salt, so freely used in the preparation of almost every kind of food, contains a very large amount of calcareous earthy matter and produces great damage to the body economy.

The theory is that the gradual accumulation of earthy salts in the system is the result of Old Age. Investigation shows that it is just the reverse. It is the cause of Old Age.

If the number of years man lives causes the ossification that accompanies Old Age, then, as like causes produces like affects, all of the same age should show the same state of ossification. Investigation shows this is not so. It is common to find people of fifty who are as weak and decrepit as others are at 75 or 80.

Years ago an English doctor wrote:

"Age is an evil that is not at all inevitable. It is not a question of dates and birthdays, but a matter of natural tendencies and dispositions. The age of the body is irrelevant so long as its condition remains young. Youth is not a time of life, but a quality, a trait of character, a mental and physical state."

In youth the organs and structures are elastic, pliable, and yielding; the senses are keen, the mind active. In Old Age these qualities are usurped by rigidity, ossification. The senses are lacking in susceptibility, the mind in memory.

In Old Age the arteries have thickened walls and are smaller in caliber, caused by fibrinous, gelatinous and earthy deposits. Thus the blood supply to the organs grows less and less, hence their deterioration and the failing of their functions.

Hardening and thickening of the blood vessels is not the work of Time, but of the earthy matter deposited by the blood-and the condition increases year by year, unless one changes one's habits.

Analysis shows that the blood holds in solution the earthy salts, the calcareous and osseous substances of the same kind as the solidifying agents, and arterial blood contains more than venous. This shows that each cycle of the blood leaves deposits of these damaging agents. It is the common carrier that clogs the system. but its supply must be replenished. Whence comes the new supply? From air, food and drink, from drugs and medicines. There is no other source.

FRUITS HAVE LITTLE EARTHY MATTER

We are dealing here with vegetables and cereals. Water and air will be noticed in due course. Writers have little to say about water in this respect, and nothing about air. Evans writes:

"If man subsists on food that contains a large proportion of lime, a large proportion will enter into the composition of the chyme, the chyle, and the blood; and as from the blood the deposition of lime takes place, the greater the amount of lime that the blood contains, the greater will be the amount deposited in the system, the greater the degree of ossification, and the sooner will be produced that rigidity, inactivity and decrepitude which make him old and bring him to premature death.

"On the other hand, if the food and drink are selected from the articles that contain the least amount of lime, the lead amount will enter into the composition of the chime, the chyle, and the blood, the less amount there will be to deposit, the less degree of ossification, the less the rigidity, inactivity, and decrepitude, and the longer the life of man,

Dr. Evans says:

"The cereals constitute the basis of modern man's food. They contain large quantities of mineral matter and, as a class, are the worst adapted as food for man, in regard to long life. Bread, man's so-called 'staff of life' is, to a great extent, the cause of his premature death (p.290).

Evans gives over twenty pages of tables of the analysis of foods, which show that fruits and nuts have the least proportion of earthy matter, as compared with their nourishing properties, of any of the foods now used by man. Next in order are animal foods, then come vegetables, and last are the pulses and cereals, which are shown to have the largest amount of earthy matter. Evans then observes.

"From the foregoing analysis we see that fruits, as distinct from vegetables, have the least amount of earthy matter. Most of them contain a large amount of water, but that water in itself is the purest kind – a distilled water of Nature."

After quoting many authors on the subject, Dr. Evans says:

"We have traced to the blood these earthy compounds that are found in the system and which increase as age advances. By the process of transpiration, they are gradually deposited by the blood. From the blood we trace them to the chyle, from the chyle to the chyme, from the chyme, from the chime to the contents of the stomach, and thence to the articles of diet. Thus we eat to live, and we eat to die." (...How to Prolong Life, P. 28).

Evans filled many pages to show that food hardens and clogs the tissues and blood vessels, causing decrepitude and death. That is excellent evidence to prove that eating is not natural. If we grow decrepit and die because of something we do, then we should not do that thing.

In the light of late nutritional discoveries, it appears more correct to say--as we eat to live, we actually eat to die.

FRESH FRUIT

So long as man must eat, the best food is fresh fruits, berries and melons. These contain fluid of the best and purest kind, distilled by natural processes.

Some of these fruit juices are a wonderful solvent, opening the way into capillaries already clogged and hardened, provided the process has not gone too far.

One author says that with a course of fresh grape juice, people with sunken eyes, wrinkled skin, and poor complexion have made surprising improvement in recovering a younger appearance.

CARNIVORISM IS BAD

"In nature a curious yet simple phenomenon is often observed... a rise and fall. If perpetual, it alternates and becomes a fall and rise. Man has degenerated. This degeneration is due solely to his diet. He has fallen; but we hope that he has risen to the highest point in the art of shortening his days, and that in the present generation he will commence gradually to fall back on his original and ordained diet. Since the creation, the days of man's existence have been little by little decreasing—it has been a gradual fall; but both science and religion tell us that he must rise again, that his life on earth must be prolonged," Dr. Charles W. De Lacy Evans in How to Prolong Life, 1879.

Evans made that statement seventy-two years ago. Were he alive today, he would see that has not yet commenced to fall back on his original and ordained diet—fuits and nuts. He is also in error when he says that man's degeneration is due solely to diet.

For more than half a century we have read book after book on food and feeding and have closely followed the explanations and arguments. We found that those who favored Vegetarianism omitted all the bad features, and the same course was pursued by those who favored carnivorism.

Books favoring Vegetarianism are composed by prejudiced authors who say nothing of the damaging qualities of vegetables and cereals. Those favoring carnivorism are composed by authors who carefully omit the changing properties of flesh.

Such authors do much damage by giving their readers half truths. A half truth can be more dangerous than a lie, as it is more misleading. We will be soundly criticized by all hands for giving the facts as we find them.

One author writes:

"The food of the natives of New Zealand and many South Sea Islands consists of fish, flesh, fowls, eggs, fruits, berries, leaves and sea-weeds, all of which contain a comparatively small amount of earthy matter. They are healthy and energetic beyond the age of 100 years and are said to be equal to the finest young men in Europe after they have reached 100 years of age." (P.268).

We do not question thee statements. But it is important to note that the instances of longevity mentioned occurred in the cases of those who lived in regions remote from the centers of civilization and are free of the degrading influences and polluted air of such centers. We shall observe in due course some of the unnoticed dangers of polluted air that are striking people down in civilization at an alarming rate.

These South Sea Islanders live a more natural life, breathe better air, and subsist on a diet that damages the body less than the conventional diet of civilization. If these natives, in their favorable environment, ate only fruits and berries, it would no doubt double and perhaps triple their present life-span.

BUTTER, MILK AND CHEESE LESS HARMFUL

The early Greek historian Herodotus told of a people of Ethiopia who, because of their unusual longevity, were called Macrobians. Their diet consisted entirely of roasted flesh and milk, both of which contain only a small amount of earthy matter. They were remarkable for their "beauty and the large proportion of their body, in each of which they surpassed other men," he wrote. They lived to be 120 and some to be much older (Densmore, P. 268).

Fishermen and those living near the sea who subsist chiefly on fish have good health and live to considerable ages.

Fowls that subsist chiefly on fish and flesh, as the pelican, vulture, hawk, eagle, owl, have much longer life-spans than domesticated fowls, as chickens, turkeys, and pigeons fed large qualities of grain.

According to Captain Riley, some tribes of Arabs of the desert, subsisting entirely on the milk of their camels, have no sickness nor disorders, and attain to great age, with remarkable vigor and vitality. He wrote:

"I am fully of the opinion that a great many Arabs on this vast desert live to an age of 200 years and more. Their lives are regular from birth to death; their climate dry and unchangeable; they are not subject to hard labor, yet have sufficient exercise for the purpose of heath."

Camel's milk contains little earthy matter and does little damage to the body; the people are not subject to the hard manual labor of the toilers of civilization, the climate of their region is not changeable; their lives are regular; and, more important, the Breath of life they inhale is not polluted with the poisons of civilization.

John Smith gives cites the case of Ephraim Pratt, of Shutesbury, who died in 1804 at the age of 116. For forty years he lived very much on milk, and yet he could "mow a good swath" almost up to the day of his death (p. 275).

Smith mentions the case of "Paul the hermit" who lived to be 115. He spent nearly a century in the desert and lived largely on dates and water. Also, the case of a shepherd at Gompus, Hungary, who lived to be 126. He "subsisted entirely on milk, butter and cheese, and was never ill." (P.277) But in those days "pasteurized" milk was unknown.

While the articles of diet such as milk, butter and cheese are less harmful than many other things men eat, they are not suitable for the body. Science finds that one cause of hardened blood vessels and tissues is the cholesterin contained in milk, eggs, butter and cheese.

One scientist says:

"Hardening of the arteries, which has been experimentally produced by other agents such as a high protein diet of whole wheat, is undoubtedly due chiefly to the deposit of cholesterin along their interior walls.

"Also, it is an interesting fact that just as the excess of cholesterin in the senile organism causes the characteristic symptoms of arterio-sclerosis, so it causes the increased incidence of cancers, tumors and carcinomas at this stage of life.

"Every other animal except man is weaned in infancy, but man continues drinking milk or using it in foods all his life. Very few animals eat eggs, and then only during the three or four weeks egg-laying season, but man eats them all year round all his life.

"Cholesterin is an animal fat found in meats, fish, fowl, eggs, lard, butter, milk,, cream and cheese, Hence the first offensive in the attack on all disorders of old age must be a diet that excludes the animal products just mentioned."

The paradox that man eats to live and eats to die explains itself as we proceed. A child can understand that if a man lives 200 years on a diet of camel's milk, or dates ad water, and only 50 on a diet of flesh, cereals and vegetables, the difference in the life-span depends chiefly on the difference in the diet and the other factors enumerated, such as climate, air, labor.

We should not make the mistake of giving diet all the credit, as most writers do. Under the same circumstances, it is possible for man to live 200 years along with these Arabs, eating the foods of civilization, provided he keep down to a minimum the amount consumed so the body is able to handle it.

In due course we shall cite cases of men who have lived up to 256 years, and their great ages did not depend entirely on the food they ate.

REASON FOR INCREASON VITALITY

Now for some facts concealed by the authors who favor Canivorism and believe that a diet of fish, flesh and milk is responsible for the remarkable longevity of those who subsist on these substances.

Animal food possesses a greater proportion of stimulating power to its quantity of nutriment matter than vegetables and cereals. For that reason it accelerates all the functions of the system, rendering vital changes quicker and less complete, and the general result of the vital economy less perfect.

Moore demonstrated at the Harvard Laboratories of Physiology that a diet of flesh produces acceleration of heart action that is surprising in the magnitude and duration.

After a meal of meat, the increase in heart rate regularly amounts to 25 to 50 percent rise above the fasting level and persists, in experimental subjects, for 15 to 20 hours, to reach a total of many thousands of extra heart beats.

As the heart beats in harmony with the blood flow, this shows how much faster a stimulating flesh diet makes the blood move and the body organs work, as their work keeps pace with the blood stream.

The findings of Moore were confirmed by Dr. Arthur Hunter, actuary of the New York Life Insurance Company. His investigation showed that flesh eating quickens body function, heart action, and raises blood pressure.

It requires the presence of internal poisons to cause the body functions to quicken in this manner.

The stimulating effect that appears to result from flesh rises from the rapid decay of the flesh. The flesh decaying in the digestive tract forms some of the most deadly poisons known to chemists. The body intelligence senses the danger and knows the poisons must be eliminated quickly to minimize the damage to the tissues and organs. So the speed of all functions is increased to cast out the dangerous enemy as soon as possible.

We now meet another paradox. The quickened functions make the man feel stronger, and he gives credit for it to the flesh he ate. He is right, but how ignorant he is of the price he pays for the temporary increase of vitality.

There is no law of organic life, extending over the whole animal and vegetal kingdom, more general and more certain than this: The slower the growth of organic bodies, consistently with the healthy and vigorous condition and action of the vital powers, the more complete are the vital processes, and the more perfect and symmetrical is the general development.

In the vital economy of the human body, all the changes concerned in the development and maintenance of the system are the most healthfully slow and complete when the food consists of fruits.

It follows from every known physiological principle in the human constitution that all other things being equal—a diet of fruit is most conducive to the completeness of bodily development and perfectness of symmetry and beauty.

FLESH FOODS PUTREFY

The rapid transformation of the tissues in the Carnivora is a condition of their existence. It is only as the result of the change of matter in the body that its vital organs are the better protected from the damage resulting from the poisons generated by decaying flesh in the bowels and blood.

Another fact is worthy of observation in connection with our subject. So far as chemical tests are concerned, the chyle of all animals is the same, from whatever kind of food it may be formed. But as to its physiological qualities and its relations to the vital economy, its character varies with the foods consumed.

Physiologists unite in stating that chyle formed from flesh food will putrefy in three or four days at the longest, while chyle formed from vegetable food, because of its greater purity; may be kept for many days without becoming putrid.

They find that human blood formed of flesh food will putrefy, when taken from the living blood-vessel, in a much shorter time than that formed of vegetal aliment; and that, other things being equal, there is always a greater febrile and putrescent tendency in the living body of those who subsist largely on flesh than in those who subsist wholly on vegetables.

If two healthy, robust men of the same age, the one subsisting mostly on flesh and the other exclusively on vegetables and water, he suddenly shot and killed in warm weather, and both bodies be laid out in the usual manner, and left to the action of the elements, the body of the vegetarian will remain two or three times as long as the body of the flesh-eater without becoming intolerably offensive from the process of putrefaction. This fact was fully confirmed by Majendia.

It may here be noticed that the excretions from the lungs, skin, kidneys and alimentary canal of the Herbivors are far less offensive than those of the Carnivora. We know from this that the breath, perspiration, body odor, etc. of the vegetarian are not so unpleasant as those of him who eats flesh food.

From the foregoing facts it may be concluded that the more rapidly the changes in the chyle of the Carnivora, the more rapid is the state of ossification, hardening, stiffening of the body. All processes of bodily decay are accelerated and the approach of Old Age is hastened.

Hence, a diet of flesh is less favorable to health and longevity than one of fruits and nuts, which form chyle and blood less subject to chemical decomposition, and require less rapid changes.

Hufeland said.

“The more slowly man grows, the later he attains maturity; and the longer all his powers are in expanding, the longer will be the duration of his life. It is natural law that the life of a creature is lengthened in proportion to the time required for growth and development.”

MODE OF LIVING BUILDS CRAVINGS, ACHES AND PAINS

Most of the stimulating effect of flesh food rises from its rapid decay in the stomach, bowels, and blood. The body strives to protect itself by an increase of its functions in order to eliminate the poisonous and quickly as possible. As this is continued year and after year, the victim is hurried to the grave.

Haig said:

"Seventy-five percent of the most terrible disorders from which men suffer rise from poisonings of unnatural food. In a way that there is no misunderstanding, Nature says that man is a frugivorian and not a carnivorian."

Another authority states that flesh as food is more dangerous for man than nicotine, because nicotine is a single poison while flesh contains either dangerous poisons. He adds:

"According to the universal statistics on morality made by Westwards, in England, where flesh is the people's article of food, only one in every 100,000 lives to the age of 107. Of 100,000 new-born children, 30,000 die in their first year and 11,000 in their second.

"This extraordinary high rate of infant mortality has only one cause; The complete intoxication of the mother's organism which poison the child while still in embryo, "Cosmotherapy P. 284.

The flesh-eating man is in a constant state of mild irritation, intoxication, rising from the excessive stimulation caused by the poisons of the decaying flesh food in his stomach, bowels and blood.

This man has been a flesh-eater from childhood, and the condition is deep-seated and chronic. His body and organs are adjusted to it. As his nerves and brain began to be comparatively free of the intoxicating effects, of course he does not feel right. The brain and nerves begin to call for their regular stimulant; they are used to it, adapted to it, and crave it. If the flesh and coffee and toast come not at the accustomed time, they protest.

Alcoholic intoxication is that state in which the poison dulls the brain and nerves. Polluted air produces the same deadly effect. So does any poison if it is powerful enough, or enough of it is taken.

The flesh-eater, coffee and coke drinker, the smoker—they are all in a state of chronic autointoxication. When deprived of their indulgences, the effects begin to wear off, and nerves wake up. Then trouble starts.

The flesh-eater, coffee and coke drinker, the smoker--they are all in a state of chronic autointoxication. When deprived of their indulgences, the effects begin to wear off, and the nerves wake up. The trouble starts.

If the condition of autointoxication is mild, the symptoms are mild. If advanced, the symptoms are stronger and give the victims more trouble.

The sensations of hunger, uneasiness, nervousness, weakness are the symptoms of the protesting nerves as they begin to revive from their chronically poisoned state.

The trouble frightens the victim, and he sees his doctor, who administers another poison to dull and weakness the protesting nerves. That stops the symptoms and "cures" the patient.

When the body becomes adjusted to this chronic condition, it cries out for the stimulating poisons which keep it in that state. It craves them; it must have them. The nerves protest when the stimulating poisons are not forthcoming. Then a substitute is given in the shape of a drug and serum poisons.

We build the world in which we live. To change our world, we must change ourselves. Our mode of living builds our cravings, aches and pains. We should know our bad habits and conquer them. We should know what to eat and drink, how to live in harmony with cosmic law--and live accordingly. There is no substitute.

48 MILLION HAVE TRICHINOSIS

We have heard of trichinosis, Trichinella Spiralis is a parasite that imbeds itself in the muscular tissues of animals in the form of encysted worms. They infest dogs, cats, rats, hogs and other animals, live on garbage and decaying animal and vegetal matter. The worms get into the bodies of people who eat pork not cooked sufficiently to kill them.

A recent article in the Therapeutic Digest stated that, through a special technique that shows up trichinosis, post-mortems have shown that in Cleveland 35% of the inhabitants had trichinosis when they died; 24% in Washington; 31% in Minneapolis and Rochester; 43% in San Francisco; 49% in Boston; and that 48 million people in the nation have trichinosis.

If you must eat flesh and do not want worms working in your body, have your flesh well cooked to kill the worms. It is better to have the worms dead in your body than alive.

We do not recommend flesh eating, but as one moves back to a diet of fresh fruit, one may use pasteurized milk, cheese and butter, without salt, until these may be discarded entirely. These substances are products of the vital processes and do the body less damage than vegetables and cereals. No salt should ever be used on anything.

Henry S. Graves, U.S. Forest Service, wrote:

"To primitive man the forest furnished both food and shelter. Later, when he became a meat – eater, he left the forest for the treeless plains, where he found in abundance the animals upon which he preyed." (Mentor, June, 1918).

One writer says:

"During the Moon Period, man was fed upon the milk of Nature. Cosmic food was absorbed by him, and the use of the milk of animals has a tendency to put him in contact with the cosmic forces."

The real milk of Nature is that contained in fresh fruits, berries, and coconuts. Man should change to this diet as soon as practicable, and then move on to Breatharianism by gradually reducing the amount of food and liquid ingested, and getting into the good air of the hills and forests.

TABLE SALT

Common table salt is a compound of sodium and chloride, a mineral in inorganic form that cannot be used by the animal body. It enters the body as salt and leaves it as salt.

Salt is a deadly irritant to all the tissues of the body. Put some salt in your eye and feel the distressing effect.

Salt in food irritates the membrane of the stomach, and for protection, mucus is excreted by the cells. The salt passes to the bowels, the membrane of which pours out more mucus for protection; in time a catarrhal condition results.

Any substance that irritates the body cells causes the mucous membrane to excrete mucus for protection and creates a catarrhal condition in time, no matter whether it be salt, polluted air, vinegar, spices or by other irritating substance.

Salt irritates the cells, and they call for water to allay the irritation. This creates abnormal thirst and results in a water-logged body.

As the salt irritates the cells year after year, the cells and tissues harden, the blood vessels harden, the blood pressure rises, with its train of troubles.

Some of the salt is filtered from the blood by the kidneys; and in time the irritation of the salt creates a condition in the kidneys termed Bright's disease.

Haig proved that salt impedes the elimination of uric acid, which thus paves the way for gout, sciatica, rheumatism, lumbago--all symptoms arising from the use of salt and treated as "diseases."

As you get older, the flavor of food changes because the use of salt, spices and condiments has dulled the delicate taste buds of buds of the tongue and weakened your sense of taste. Salt eaters say unsalted food tastes "flat." It depends on what one is used to.

No carnivorous animal in its native state uses salt, except as an acquired habit. Animals form bad habits as man does.

OPINIONS ON SALT EATING

The North American Indians used no salt when discovered by the Europeans. Chinese in the interior of their country use no salt. Most of the human race that subsists chiefly on vegetable food uses no salt.

Dr. J. E. Cummins wrote:

"I knew of a case of a little girl who had a craving for salt. She would take a teaspoonful of it at a time when not watched. She was a pinched-faced little thing and had hardening of the arteries, was wrinkled and appeared old at the age of four years."

"Fresh flesh, over which salt is strewn, is found swimming in brine after 24 hours, yet not a drop of water has been added. The water has been yielded by the flesh itself."

Dr. Bouchon observed:

"Salt is one of the worst of social poisons. Because of its use, surgeons are constantly operating for appendicitis, gastric ulcers, and liver and kidney calculus. It atrophies, dries up or hardens the tissues, and causes persons with tendencies to arthritism to become stout and those of lymphatic temperaments to become thin." Nouville Review

Dr. Hal Bieler stated:

"Haig showed that in animals, such as dogs, and in fowls, such as Chicken, where a good deal of nitrogen is eliminated as uric acid as the result of feeding salt, even in very small quantities, the creatures soon die. Autopsy showed the liver and kidneys studded with uric acid concretions.

"Our forefathers used a salt solution as an embalming fluid. The ancient Egyptians used oils, spices and salt in their mummy wrappings. Today we mummify the living with salad dressings made of mineral oils, spice and salt. You see these mummies walking the streets. The dry skin, shrunken bodies and faded hair bespeak the hardened livers and sclerotic kidneys. It is hardly necessary to embalm such bodies after they are dead, for they are already pickled to the gills.

"The action of salt on hogs, rabbits, etc., is to paralyze the muscles of the hind quarters and the animal sinks to the ground. Later the muscles of the lungs are and the victim dies of asphyxia. If this is the result of the consumption of salt by animals, it is reasonable to support that salt has a similar affect on men--Philosophy of Health.

Dr. A. Birchard said:

> "Man is the only animal that deliberately commits suicide by self poisoning. He is the only animal that spoils his food before he eats it. The average individual suffers constantly from chronic poisoning of some kind, due to the food he eats, either in wrong combination or in excessive amounts, or by adding to it injurious substances to stimulate a jaded appetite.
>
> "Instead of fasting until he has no appetite for the best of foods, he tries to create an appetite by the use of irritating and injurious condiments, or he does himself with various sorts of poisons.

"He usually begins the day with a poison dose, in the form of coffee, to wake him up, or may be a drink of whisky or bitters to produce an appetite. Probably he finds an afternoon cup of tea necessary to relieve after-dinner stupor. At night he needs a narcotic to put him to sleep; and in the morning, a cathartic to move his bowels.

"With all his other poisonings, he spoils his food by putting into it toxic substances which, by means of acrid, biting and burning flavors, belong to the poison class and are unfit to eat. These poisonous substances, used only for their flavoring properties and having no food value, are known as condiments. -Philosophy of Health.

Another eminent author states:

"Wild boars and other mammals exceed the age of 200 years because they instinctively follow a natural diet. It is only man who eats everything indiscriminately. He arranges his meals by the clock (due too the artificial life he lives; and thus his hunger is only a form of habit and not a form of natural hunger." --Cosmotherapy, p. 280.

The fact that man lives as long as he does in his artificial state, called civilization, is an indication of his hardiness and toughness.

Barrel-Chested Indians

Science Digest of January - 1957 carried a brief story of “Big Chested Indians (who) Live in High Andes” in Peru, South America.

They are small; the average male is about five feet tall and weighs only 114 pounds. They live at altitudes up to 11,000 feet in the mountains, and their chief articles of food are said to be potatoes and corn.

The people have tremendous chests, which permit them to inhale sufficient air for heavy work. They customarily trot along difficult mountain trials carrying heavy burdens. For sport, they stage races in which they run with 150—pound sacks of potatoes on their backs.

The account states that they are “being studied by scientists from the U.S. and Peru.”

Nothing will come out of this study that will in any way have an adverse effect on the orthodox mode of living in this civilization.

The report of these scientists will not say that long life and good health are the natural products of living on a simple diet in a warm region where frost and freeze are unknown – the natural home of man.

The press of Oct. 22, 1956, stated that William Bisset, of Port Elizabeth, South Africa, was 160 years old and the doctors who examined him found him in good health and with an excellent memory.

The press of 1956 contained numerous accounts of the man from Columbia, South America, named Javier Pereira, who is 167 years old. He was brought to the United States to be studied by scientists in an effort to learn the secret of his long life.

We do not search in the stone for the reason why it falls to the earth when cast into the air. The secret of Pereira's long life lays in the environment where he lived, in the climate, and in his habits.

The press of November 13, 1956, stated that Mrs. Maria Garzon Cuida de' Casteneda, who also lived in Colombia, South America, was 178 years old and in good health. She was born December 30, 1778, two years after the signing of the Declaration of Independence of the United States.

While these natives of the tropics are living well over the century mark, the health officers of this country are dying in their forties and fifties.

Made in the USA
Las Vegas, NV
21 July 2025

25164984R00056